Copyright © 2019 by Scott W. Holmes

All rights reserved. No part of this book may be reproduced or used in any manner without written permission of the copyright owner except for the use of quotations with credit to the author.

For more information, address:
Scott_Holmes@Cate.org

FIRST EDITION

TABLE OF CONTENTS

Acknowledgements

Preface

Chapter 1: Getting coins from a bank

Chapter 2: Cents or "Pennies"

Chapter 3: Nickels

Chapter 4: Dimes

Chapter 5: Quarters

Chapter 6: Half Dollars

Chapter 7: Dollar Coins

Chapter 8: Grading Simplified

Chapter 9: Storing your finds

Chapter 10: Selling your finds

Chapter 11: 3 ways to save money while coin roll hunting

Chapter 12: FAQ's (Frequently Asked Questions)

Thank you to Dan Estes of Estes Collectible Investments.

You are a great numismatist and an even better friend.

Thank you for everything that you do.

Preface: What is coin roll hunting?

Coin Roll hunting is, simply put, an easy way to acquire coins of metals as well as numismatic (collectible) value for their face value. It is an easy and fun way for anyone to spend an afternoon. Almost everyone in the United States lives within a few miles of a bank, so all you have to do is go to that bank and buy some coins at face value to look through. Another great thing about coin roll hunting is that it costs nothing other than time. For example, if you go through $100 in nickels and you find nothing of any value, you just roll the coins backup and cash them in at a bank!

Coin roll hunting is not a new phenomenon, as people have been searching through their pocket change for decades in hopes of finding rare and valuable coins, or, more often, to complete a collection of coins. This started in 1965, when the quarter and the dime went from a composition of 90% silver, 10% copper to a composition 75% copper, 25% nickel composition, and the half dollar's silver content went from 90% to 40%. The government assured the general public that the silver coins would continue to circulate alongside the new copper-nickel coins. This, however, did not prevent people from saving rolls of these silver coins, which have appreciated in substantially in the last decade. Even before the composition of the dime, quarter, and half dollar changed, "Penny Boards" started the phenomenon of searching through pocket change.. These boards existed for pennies and have now come to encompass all circulating United States coins. Each folder is for a specific series and has a hole for each date and mintmark of that specific series. These "Penny Boards" became popular in the 1920's, as people could complete them by searching through pocket change. There was a certain level of satisfaction in completing a set of coins, and dealers payed a premium for complete sets. Though very few dealers still pay a premium for folders complete with modern coins, these folders still play a relatively big role in coin collecting today, especially in the collections of beginners.

This book outlines the kind of coins you should look for in every denomination of United States coins, from the penny to the dollar, as well as what coins are the most profitable, and, most importantly, how to deal with bank policies and tellers. When you are first beginning a coin roll hunt, don't hesitate to consult this book. All said and done, coin roll hunting is one of the best ways for collectors to acquire coins of numismatic and metallic worth for face value, and this book will help you make the most of your change

Chapter 1: Getting coins from a bank

Before you can even begin to coin roll hunt, you must first get to the bank and purchase coins. This involves many different variables, including bank policies, the amount of money you have, and, especially, the mood of the teller you are dealing with. In this chapter, I will talk you through the steps of acquiring the coins you need to hunt.

Transportation, or lack of it, is what sometimes stops younger coin roll hunters. Gas money also plays a big roll for those who can drive. My recommendation is to walk to your local bank. If you live within a mile of a town, you most likely live within a mile of a bank. I recommend that you bring a backpack and some water, as coins can be very difficult to carry for a long period of time. By walking to the bank, you will save money on gas and get good exercise. If you live further than a mile, it is best that you drive. The average car gets about 23.6 mpg[1], which means that a 5 to 6 mile round trip drive costs about $.60 to $.70 at the current average gas price of $2.79[2].

    First, and foremost, be nice. The nicer you are, the better the people at the bank will treat you. When you first enter a bank, go to the teller who seems to be in the best mood. If a bank teller is in a good enough mood, they will go to extremes to try to help you find what you are looking for. Start your conversation with the teller by explaining what you are looking for. Most tellers, after working at a bank for a little while, have a general idea of what is usual change and what is unusual change. Begin your conversation by asking the

---

[1] Plumer, Brad. "Cars in the U.S. Are More Fuel-efficient than Ever. Here's How It Happened." The Washington Post. December 13, 2013. Accessed July 23, 2019. https://www.washingtonpost.com/news/wonk/wp/2013/12/13/cars-in-the-u-s-are-more-fuel-efficient-than-ever-heres-how-it-happened/?utm_term=.b320475e2b4a.
[2] Johnson, David. "Gas Prices: See How Much More You Will Pay This Year." Time. June 12, 2018. Accessed July 23, 2019. https://time.com/5306658/gas-prices-calculator/.

teller if he or she has seen anything unusual, silver, old, etc. Chances are that they haven't, but, if you ask enough, you will eventually get that one who has. Also, understand that some tellers set aside coins for themselves. Being a bank teller is not the highest paying job in the world, so you will encounter some who put any valuable coins that they see to the side.

If, and most often when, the teller says they have nothing rare, ask if they have any half dollars. Even if you only have enough money in your pocket to buy a box of pennies, $25, half dollars can still be your money maker. Most tellers will have a few in their coin tray and, if you are lucky, may also have some rolls of half dollars. If they have no rolls of half dollars, ask to look at the ones in their tray. 99.9% of the time they will allow you to go through them. Though it is rare, every so often you will find a silver half dollar in the coin tray of a teller.

Once you have seen all of the half dollars the bank you are at has to offer and you are sure that none of them contain silver, go to your denomination of choice. Ask the teller if you can have a box of whatever denomination you intend to coin roll hunting. Most banks will be very surprised by your request for 2,000 quarter or 4,000 nickels, so ready yourself to explain why you want them. Most banks are able to spare a box of the denomination you want, but, if you are looking to pick up multiple boxes of different denominations, find a big branch. The bigger the branch, the more boxes of coins they will have in their vaults. If your bank is not able to fill your coin roll hunting needs, as if they can order you some coins. Most banks are able to place orders for their customers.

"Do you have an account here?" This is a common question posed when you are asking to buy large quantities of coin from a bank. If the teller does not ask this, do not bring it up! Bringing up the fact that you don't have an account with a teller is a sure way to increase the chance that you will not be getting any coins. Many banks have a limit on the amount of money in coins you can take from a bank per day, but there are some banks who will not sell any coins to non-customers. If you go to a bank where you are not a customer, be ready to visit another one because you might not get what you want.

The Great Debate: Customer wrapped vs. Machine wrapped

Among coin roll hunters, this is one of the biggest arguments. Everybody wants to know, or thinks they know, which one yields better results. In the next two paragraphs, I will outline the differences between the two and the advantages and disadvantages that come with both of them.

Customer wrapped coins are a less dependable option when compared to machine wrapped coins. Customer rolls turned in by another coin roll hunter will hold nothing of any value, and you can never be certain whether or not you are looking through rolls of coins from a change jar or the discarded contents of a coin roll hunters. Then again, you have to remember that the only thing you are risking when searching through customer wrapped rolls is time. Even if the rolls contain nothing of value, all of the coins in them will always be worth the face value that you paid for them! In conclusion, if you are willing to risk not finding anything in return for the increased chance of finding something truly exceptional, I recommend you buy customer wrapped rolls. Just remember that they probably will not be available in as large a quantity as the machine wrapped rolls banks usually order from the Federal Reserve.

Machine wrapped rolls are the most dependable of the two types. You can be assured that the contents of machine wrapped rolls have never been searched through, as they come from the Federal Reserve banks. This means that they are dependable, which can be good or bad. When coin roll hunting machine-wrapped coins, you will almost always end up with close to or the same number of finds. Though it is possible to find exceptional coins on occasion, I recommend that you hunt customer wrapped rolls if you want consistency and money over time.

What are Mint marks?

Mint marks are one of the biggest factors in determining a coins value, along with grade and date. A coin may be worth $20 with a D mintmark, but $3000 dollars with a CC mint mark. Below I will outline what mint marks are and what they signify. I will also explain what each mintmark stands for.

First off, you must understand that a mintmark is a certain mints stamp. A mintmark tells you where the coin was produced. Mint marks help the government keep track of how many coins each mint is producing. By doing this, the government can then look at the demand for coins from the population, and decide how many coins each mint should produce.

Today, there are only four cities with operating mints: Philadelphia, Pennsylvania; Denver, Colorado; San Francisco, California; and West Point, New York. West Point only produces proof coins, not coins for general circulation.. But there have been many more mints, as is outlined in the reference section of this book. Below is a list of the mint marks you may encounter in circulation, along with the location of the mint they come from and how long the mints were in operation. Also given is an example of the mintmark on a coin in photographic form.

The P mintmark designates the Philadelphia mint, which is one of the four remaining United States mints and has been operational since 1793. An example of a coin with a P mintmark as well as a coin entirely without a mintmark are shown below.

"Lincoln Wheat Cent." USA Coin Book. Accessed July 21, 2019.
https://www.usacoinbook.com/coins/small-cents/lincoln-wheat-cent/.

The above coin is from the Philadelphia mint, but does not have the "P" mintmark that designates the Philadelphia mint.

"2017 P Lincoln Shield Cent Small Cents Copper Plated Zinc Penny." USA Coin Book. Accessed July 21, 2019. https://www.usacoinbook.com/coins/6036/small-cents/lincoln-shield-cent/2017-P/.

The above coin is from the Philadelphia mint and has the "P" mintmark below the date on the obverse that designates the Philadelphia mint.

The D mintmark comes from Denver, Colorado. The Denver mint is one of the four remaining United States mints, and has been operational since 1897. An example of a coin minted at the Denver mint is shown below.

"1943 D Jefferson Nickels Wartime Composition." USA Coin Book. Accessed July 21, 2019. https://www.usacoinbook.com/coins/998/nickels/jefferson/1943-D/.

The above coin is from the Denver mint and has the D mint mark above Monticello on the reverse. The D designates the Denver Mint.

The S mint mark comes from San Francisco, California. The San Francisco mint is one of the four remaining United States mints, and has been operational since 1869. An example of a coin with an S mintmark is shown below.

"1901 S Barber Quarters Early Silver Quarters." USA Coin Book. Accessed July 21, 2019.
https://www.usacoinbook.com/coins/1947/quarters/barber/1901-S/

The above coin was minted in the San Francisco mint. It has the "S" mintmark that designates a coin that has been minted at the San Francisco mint. The "S" mint mark appears below the tail feathers of the eagle on the reverse.

The O mint mark comes from New Orleans, Louisiana. The New Orleans mint no longer produces coins, but it was operational from 1838 until 1861, and then again from 1879 until 1909. An example of a coin with an O mint mark is shown below.

"1907 O Barber Dimes Early Silver Dimes." USA Coin Book. Accessed July 21, 2019. https://www.usacoinbook.com/coins/1443/dimes/barber/1907-O/.

The above coin was minted by the New Orleans mint. It has the "O" mint mark that designates a coin that has been minted by the New Orleans mint. The "O" mint mark appears below the wreath on the reverse of the coin.

The CC mint mark comes from Carson City, Nevada. The Carson City mint is no longer operational, but it produced only silver and gold coins when it was in operation. The Carson City mint was operational from 1870 until 1899. Below is an example of a coin with a CC mintmark.

"1893 CC Morgan Dollars Early Silver Dollars." USA Coin Book. Accessed July 21, 2019. https://www.usacoinbook.com/coins/3262/dollars/morgan/1893-CC/.

The above coin was minted by the Carson City mint. It has the "CC" mint mark that designates a coin that has been minted by the Carson City mint. The "CC" mint mark appears on the reverse of the coin above the word "DOLLAR" and below the half wreath that partially surrounds the eagle.

Chapter 2: Cents or "Pennies"

Cents, or "pennies, as they are most often called, are the cheapest denomination to sort through, for obvious reasons. Pennies come in boxes of 2500, or $25. Pennies come in 50¢ rolls, so each box contains 50 rolls. Don't be disillusioned by the relatively modest face value of a box of pennies. They still take just as long to look through as any other denomination and are very heavy! A box of pennies weighs about 17 pounds!

Coins to Keep

Pennies are a relatively easy denomination to look through. When looking through pennies, you want to keep all coins from before 1959.

Wheat Cents

The majority of coins from before 1959 that you will find are going to be what are called "wheat cents". This refers to the two wheat ears that appear on the reverse of the "wheat penny" design. A picture below illustrates a common-date example of the design, as well as the location of the mintmark.

"1935 S Lincoln Wheat Cent Small Cents Bronze Composite Penny." USA Coin Book. Accessed July 21, 2019. https://www.usacoinbook.com/coins/417/small-cents/lincoln-wheat-cent/1935-S/.

Lincoln Wheat cent design, produced from 1909 until 1958. The mintmark is located below the date on the obverse of the coin.

These pennies were produced from 1909 until 1958. All of the coins from this time period are valuable, but some more than others. A regular or "common-date" Wheat cent can usually be sold for about 4 cents, or 3 cents net profit. Common-date pennies from before 1930 are worth closer to 8 cents. Below are listed some of the more rare or "key" dates in the series, ordered by date from oldest to newest.

Key dates (worth more than $50 in lower circulated

grades):

1909-S, 1909-S V.D.B. (See photos below), 1911-S, 1914-D, 1931-S

Semi-Key dates (worth more than $15 in lower circulated grades):

1910-S, 1912-S, 1913-S, 1914-S, 1915-S, 1922-D, 1924-D

"1909 S Lincoln Wheat Cent Small Cents VDB Bronze Composite Penny." USA Coin Book. Accessed July 21, 2019. https://www.usacoinbook.com/coins/343/small-cents/lincoln-wheat-cent/1909-S/vdb/.

The above image illustrates an example of a 1909-S V.D.B. Wheat cent. "V.D.B." is located on the bottom of the reverse of the coin and represents the initials of the designer of the coin, Victor D. Brenner.

Indian Head Cents

A design from before 1959 that will be much harder to find than the wheat penny design is the Indian head penny. A picture below illustrates a common-date example of the design, as well as the location of the mintmark.

"1908 S Indian Head Cent Small Cents Bronze Composite Penny." USA Coin Book. Accessed July 21, 2019. https://www.usacoinbook.com/coins/337/small-cents/indian-head-cent/1908-S/

Indian Head cent design, produced from 1859 until 1909. The mintmark is located below the wreath on the reverse of the coin.

These pennies were produced from 1859 until 1909. All Indian Head pennies are valuable and should be carefully saved! A common-date Indian head penny is usually worth between 50 cents and 1 dollar, though many coins from the series are worth much more. Below are listed some of the key-dates of the series, ordered by date from oldest to newest. Please note that all coins produced from 1859 until 1878 have a value of at least $10.

Key dates (worth more than $100 in lower circulated grades):

1877, 1908-S, 1909-S

Semi-Key dates (worth more than $25 in lower circulated grades):

1864, with L (see below), 1866, 1867, 1868, 1869, 1870, 1871, 1876, 1878

"1864 P Indian Head Cent Small Cents With L Bronze Composite Penny." USA Coin Book. Accessed July 21, 2019. https://www.usacoinbook.com/coins/281/small-cents/indian-head-cent/1864-P/with-l/.

The above image illustrates an 1864 "with L" Indian head cent. It is important to be able to distinguish between "with L" and "without L" Indian Head cents from 1864 as the difference in price can be hundreds of dollars.

Flying Eagle Cents

The last design that you might encounter when coin roll hunting through pennies is the Flying Eagle cent. Before I further explain this design, please note that finding one of these pennies in circulation is nearly impossible. I have searched through thousands of dollars in pennies and have never found a single one! But, if you are lucky enough to come across one, here is some information about this design.

"1858 P Flying Eagle Cent Small Cents Large Letters Flying Eagle Penny." USA Coin Book. Accessed July 21, 2019.
https://www.usacoinbook.com/coins/270/small-cents/flying-eagle-cent/1858-P/large-letters/.

Flying Eagle Cent design, minted from 1856 to 1858. This design was only produced at the Philadelphia mint, so there are no coins that have mintmarks.

This design was produced from 1856-1858. Coins from 1857 and 1858 are worth a little over $10 in their very worst condition. The most valuable coin from this design is the 1856 flying eagle cents. Only about 2,000 1856 flying eagle cents were produced, making it the scarcest small cent. A coin in lower circulated grades will sell for over $7500!

Profit and probability per box

Though many people do coin roll hunting because they enjoy it, there are few people who do it for the sole reason of having something fun to do. Most people are looking to have fun and make a little money on the side. Due to this fact, I have broken down the average profit for a box of pennies. Please note that these are based off my years of results, so your results may be better or worse.

Wheat cents: On average, I find 15-20 wheat cents per box, and, of these 15-20 wheat cents, about 1-2 are from before 1930.

Indian head cents: On average, I find 1 Indian head cent every $250 in pennies.

Flying eagle cents: I have never personally found a flying eagle cent, but the probability of finding one is about 1 every $10,000, or 1 for every million cents you search through.

Profit Equation on Average

If you find 20 pennies in a box, and two of them are from the 1920's, your profits will look like this:

18 wheat cents from 1930-1950 x 4 cents net profit= 72 cents net profit

2 wheat cents from 1909-1929 x 8 cents net profit= 16 cents net profit

This amounts to 88 cents total profit

As you can see, pennies are not the most profitable coins to search through, but they will pass lots of time even if you only have $10. In conclusion, I recommend that you hunt through pennies if you have a good amount of free time and are looking for more enjoyment than profit.

Chapter 3: Nickels

Nickels are the most complicated denomination to sort through. There is great debate surrounding what should be kept when looking through a box of nickels, and I know that some people will agree with what I say, but some people will want to add additional things to look for. Nickels come in boxes of 4000, or $100. Nickels come in $2 rolls, so there are 50 rolls per box. A box of nickels is very heavy, weighing about 22 pounds!

Coins to Keep

Nickels can be a slightly difficult denomination to look through for someone who has little or no numismatic knowledge. Unlike pennies, there is no specific date before which all the nickels become valuable.

<u>Jefferson Nickels</u>

The coin that you will most likely find is a silver or "war-time" nickel. Examples of both the regular Jefferson nickel design and the war nickel design are shown below.

"1939 S Jefferson Nickels Pre-War Composition." USA Coin Book. Accessed July 21, 2019.
https://www.usacoinbook.com/coins/984/nickels/jefferson/1939-S/.

Regular Jefferson nickel design, minted from 1938 to 1942 and then again from 1946 until 1964. The mintmark is located to the right of Monticello on the reverse of the above coin.

"1942 S Jefferson Nickels Wartime Composition." USA Coin Book. Accessed July 21, 2019.
https://www.usacoinbook.com/coins/995/nickels/jefferson/1942-S/.

Wartime Jefferson nickel design, minted from

1942 to 1945. The mintmark is much larger and is located above Monticello on the reverse of the above coin.

These nickels were produced from 1942-1945 and are composed of 35% silver, 56% copper, and 9% manganese. They can be distinguished from other nickels by their mintmark location, which is above Monticello on the reverse as shown above. These coins generally are worth only their silver content, which is about .05626 ounces per coin. At the time of this book, silver is holding strong at about $15 to $16 an ounce, so these coins are generally worth between 85 and 90 cents.

Along with the silver nickels above, I generally keep specific dates from the Jefferson nickel series, as it is uncommon to come across them. I recommend keeping the following dates: 1938-D, 1938-S, 1939-D, 1939-S, and 1950-D.

Buffalo Nickels

The next coin that you may encounter while looking through nickels is called a Buffalo nickel. This design earned that name from the buffalo featured prominently on the reverse of the coin. Two different reverse designs exist, and examples shown below feature both reverse designs and the mint mark location on both.

"1913 S Buffalo Nickels Indian Head Nickel - Mound Type." USA Coin Book. Accessed July 21, 2019. https://www.usacoinbook.com/coins/909/nickels/buffalo/1913-S/.

Type I Buffalo Nickel, minted only in 1913. The Bison on the reverse is standing on a mound with the mintmark located below the words "FIVE CENTS".

"1913 D Buffalo Nickels Indian Head Nickel - Line Type." USA Coin Book. Accessed July 21, 2019. https://www.usacoinbook.com/coins/911/nickels/buffalo/1913-D/.

Type II Buffalo Nickel, minted from 1913 to 1938. The Bison on the reverse is standing on flat ground, unlike the Type I reverse design. The mintmark is still located below the words "FIVE CENTS".

The Buffalo nickel was produced from 1913-1938, with the first reverse design type only produced in 1913. A problem you may encounter when you find a buffalo nickel in a roll of coins is that the date is worn off completely. Because the date is a raised or elevated part of the coin, it is not uncommon for coins that have circulated for long periods of time to have a partial date or no date at all. Coins in this condition are generally worth about 12 to 15 cents. A coin with a full date that is not a key-date coin is usually worth about 40 to 60 cents. There are also some more valuable dates from the buffalo nickel series listed below from oldest to newest..

Key dates (worth more than $50 in lower circulated grades):

1913-D, type II, 1913-S type II, 1914-D, 1915-S, 1921-S

Semi-Key dates (worth more than $20 in lower circulated grades):

1913-S, type I, 1914-S, 1915-D, 1917-D, 1917-S, 1918-D, 1926-S

Liberty Head Nickels

The two coins mentioned above are going to be the large majority of the coins that you find while searching through nickels. The third design that is rare to find, but still possible, is the liberty head nickel. Two examples are shown below, including one that shows mintmark location.

"1883 P Liberty Nickels No Cents Liberty Head." USA Coin Book. Accessed July 21, 2019. https://www.usacoinbook.com/coins/873/nickels/liberty/1883-P/no-cents/.

"Without Cents" Liberty Head nickel design. This design was minted only in 1883, and the word "CENTS" was added to the reverse of the design later that year.

"1912 D Liberty Nickels Liberty Head." USA Coin Book. Accessed July 21, 2019. https://www.usacoinbook.com/coins/904/nickels/liberty/1912-D/.

"With Cents" Liberty Head Nickel design, minted from 1883 until 1913. Notice the addition of the word "CENTS" below the wreath. The mintmark is located below the dot to the left of the word "CENTS".

Liberty head nickels were produced from 1883 until 1913, though only 5 1913 Liberty Head nickels are known to exist. If you find yourself in possession of one of these 5, you have might have robbed someone very important, or, more likely, the coin that you have is a counterfeit.. Due to the fact that only 5 liberty head nickels exist from 1913, the majority of Liberty head nickels were produced between 1883 and 1912. A common date liberty head nickel is worth between 75¢ and $1.50. As with any other design, the Liberty head nickel also has key dates which are listed from oldest to newest below.

Key dates (worth more than $150 in lower circulated grades):

1885, 1886, 1912-S

Semi-Kay dates (worth more than $20 in lower circulated grades):

1883, with cents, 1884, 1888, 1894

Shield Nickels

The next design holds about the same probability of discovery as a flying eagle cent. This design is called a Shield nickel, which refers to the shield on the front of the coin. This coin is very rare to discover in circulation, and I have never found one in circulation and do not know of anyone who has. Nevertheless, it is almost certain that some still remain in circulation. Two different reverse designs exist, and examples shown below feature both reverse designs.

"1866 P Shield Nickels With Rays Early Five Cent Nickels." USA Coin Book. Accessed July 21, 2019. https://www.usacoinbook.com/coins/850/nickels/shield/1866-P/with-rays/.

Type I Shield nickel design, minted from 1866 until halfway through 1867. The rays were removed from this design halfway through 1867

"1870 P Shield Nickels Early Five Cent Nickels." USA Coin Book. Accessed July 21, 2019. https://www.usacoinbook.com/coins/856/nickels/shield/1870-P/.

Type II Shield nickel design, minted from 1867 until 1883. The rays were removed from the Type I Shield nickel design halfway through 1867.

Shield nickels were produced from 1866 to 1883. A common-date shield nickel is worth about $10 to $15. The key dates in the series are shown below from oldest to newest.

Key dates (worth more than $150 in lower circulated grades):

1879, 1880, 1881

Semi-Key dates (worth more than $50 in lower circulated grades):

1871, 1875

Profit and probability per box

Though many people do coin roll hunting because they enjoy it, there are few people who do for the sole reason of having fun. Most people are looking to have fun and make a little money on the side. Due to this fact, I have broken down the average profit for a box of nickels. Please note that these are a general average of my years of results, so your results may be better or worse.

Silver Nickels: On average, I find 1-2 silver nickels per box of nickels.

Buffalo Nickels: On average, I find 1-2 Buffalo nickels per 2 boxes of nickels, or 0-1 nickels per box.

Liberty Head Nickels: On average, I find 1 Liberty Head nickel every $1500 in nickels.

Shield Nickels: I have never found a Shield nickel, but the probability of finding one is about 1 every $5,000, or 1 for every 100,000 nickels.

Profit Equation on Average

If you find 2 silver nickels and a buffalo nickel with

a full date in a box, your profits will look like this:

2 silver nickels x 85 cents net profit= $1.70 net profit

1 full date buffalo nickel x 45 cents net profit= 45 cents net profit

This amounts to $2.15 net profit

As you can see, nickels are much more profitable than pennies and will, through some time, earn you a substantial amount of money. I recommend nickels for anyone who is focused more on money, but still wants to enjoy themselves coin roll hunting.

Chapter 4: Dimes

Dimes are a very simple denomination to coin roll hunt. Dimes are either silver or not silver, and one is worth much more than 10 cents and the other is worth 10 cents. Dimes come in boxes of 2500 dimes, or $250. Dimes come in $5 rolls, so there are 50 rolls per box. A box of dimes is on the lighter side of the coin roll hunting weight spectrum, weighing in at about 12 pounds per box.

Coins to Keep

When searching through dimes, you want to keep every coin from before 1965, as these are composed of 90% silver.

Roosevelt Dimes

The most common design you will find with a date from before 1965 is the Roosevelt dime. Examples below illustrate the difference in mintmark placement of a silver-copper composition and a copper-nickel Roosevelt dime.

"1972 D Roosevelt Dimes Clad Composition." USA Coin Book. Accessed July 21, 2019. https://www.usacoinbook.com/coins/1618/dimes/roosevelt/1972-D/.

Copper-Nickel (75% Copper, 25% Nickel) Roosevelt dimes, minted from 1965 until present day. The mintmark is located above the date on the obverse.

"1946 D Roosevelt Dimes Silver Composition." USA Coin Book. Accessed July 21, 2019. https://www.usacoinbook.com/coins/1552/dimes/roosevelt/1946-D/.

Silver (90% Silver, 10% Copper) Roosevelt dimes, minted from 1946 until 1964. The mintmark is located to the left of the bottom of the torch on the reverse.

The Roosevelt Dime was produced with a 90% silver, 10% copper composition from 1946 until 1964. All coins after 1964 were produced with a 75% copper, 25% nickel composition, so they are worth no more than 10 cents. There are no key dates in the Roosevelt dime series, so the dimes are only really valuable because of their silver content. Roosevelt dimes contain .07234 ounces of silver, and, with silver usually hovering between $14 and $16 an ounce, they tend to be worth between $1 and $1.30.

Liberty Head "Mercury" Dimes

The second design that is commonly found when searching through dimes is the Winged Liberty Head or, as it is more commonly known, "Mercury" dime. This coin earned its name from the obverse design, which features Lady Liberty with wings attached to her head to simulate freedom of thought. Many people thought that the bust on the obverse depicted the Roman god Mercury, so the design earned the nickname "Mercury dime". Below is an example which includes mintmark location.

"Mercury Dimes." USA Coin Book. Accessed July 21, 2019. https://www.usacoinbook.com/coins/dimes/mercury/.

Liberty Head or "Mercury" dime design, minted from 1916 until 1945. The mintmark is located at

the bottom left of the *fasces* on the reverse.

The Liberty Head dime was produced from 1916 until 1945 and was composed of 90% silver, 10% copper. A common-date example of a Liberty Head dime is worth about the same as a Roosevelt dime: about $1.20 to $1.30. Unlike the Roosevelt dime series, the Mercury dime series does have some key dates, which are listed below in order of oldest to newest.

Key dates (worth more than $50 in lower circulated grades):

1916-D* (extremely rare, see below), 1921, 1921-D

Semi-Kay dates (worth more than $10 in lower circulated grades):

1926-S

*The 1916-D is the king of all Mercury dimes due to its rarity and great value. Due to this, many 1916-D's are faked, so I recommend that you send any 1916-D that you find in for certification. For more on getting coins certified, see **Chapter 8**.

Barber Dimes

A much rarer design that you might discover while coin roll hunting is called the Barber Dime. The design name refers to the chief engraver at the time who designed the coin: Charles Barber. A design example is given below, which includes mint mark location.

"Barber Dimes." USA Coin Book. Accessed July 21, 2019.
https://www.usacoinbook.com/coins/dimes/barber/.

Barber dime design, minted from 1892 until 1916. The Mintmark is located on the reverse at the bottom of the wreath.

The Barber dime was produced from 1892 until 1916. A common-date example of a Barber dime sells for a little more than its melt value, which is the same as the melt value of the Liberty

Head dime and the Roosevelt dime. A Barber dime sells for about $1.60 to $1.70, the extra 40 cents added on due to its numismatic, or collectible value. The Barber dime series also contains a few key dates, which are listed below from oldest to newest.

Key dates (worth more than $50 in lower circulated grades):

1892-S, 1894-O, 1895, 1895-O, 1896-O, 1896-S, 1897-O, 1901-S, 1903-S

Semi-Key dates (worth more than $25 in lower circulated grades):

1893-O, 1894, 1895-S, 1904-S, 1913-S

Profit and probability per box

Though many people do coin roll hunting because they enjoy it, there are few people who do it solely to have something fun to do. Most people are looking to have fun and make a little money on the side. Due to this fact, I have broken down the average profit for a box of dimes. Please note that these are based off my years of results, so your results may be better or worse.

Roosevelt Dimes: On average, I find 0-1 Roosevelt dimes per box ($250) of dimes.

Mercury Dimes: On average, I find 1 Mercury dime every 4 boxes ($1000) of dimes.

Barber Dimes: I have never found a Barber Dime in circulation, but the probability of finding one is about 1 every $5,000, or one every 50,000 dimes.

Profit Equation on Average

If you find 1 Roosevelt dime in a box of dimes, your profits will look like this:

1 Silver Roosevelt Dime x $1.20 net profit= $1.20 net profit

This amounts to a $1.20 total net profit

As you can see, dimes are profitable if you can find silver dimes large quantities, but a box of dimes is usually not incredibly profitable. I recommend dimes for someone who is looking more towards the profit side of coin roll hunting and is willing to buy, and go through, multiple boxes of coins.

Chapter 5: Quarters

Quarters are, in my opinion, the worst denomination to coin roll hunt. The chances of finding a silver quarter are very low. Quarters are still a very simple denomination, as they follow the same rules as dimes. Quarters come in boxes of 2000, or $500. Quarters come in $10 rolls, so there are 50 rolls per box. A box of quarters is pretty heavy, weighing about 23 pounds.

Coins to Keep

When searching through quarters, you want to keep every coin from before 1965, as these are composed of 90% silver, 10% copper.

Washington Quarters

The most common design example you will encounter is the Washington quarter. Examples below illustrate the difference in mintmark placement of a silver-copper composition and a copper-nickel Washington quarter.

"1971 D Washington Quarters Clad Composition." USA Coin Book. Accessed July 21, 2019. https://www.usacoinbook.com/coins/2135/quarters/washington/1971-D/.

Copper-Nickel (75% Copper, 25% Nickel) Washington quarter design minted from 1965 until present. The Mintmark is located to the left of Washington's bust on the obverse.

"Washington Quarters." USA Coin Book. Accessed July 21, 2019. https://www.usacoinbook.com/coins/quarters/washington/.

Silver (90% silver, 10% copper) Washington quarter design minted from 1932 until 1964. The mintmark is located above the words "QUARTER DOLLAR" on the lower portion of the reverse.

The Washington quarter was produced with a 90% silver, 10% copper composition from 1946 until 1964. All coins after 1964 were produced with a 75% copper, 25% nickel composition, so they are worth no more than 25 cents. All Washington quarters contain .1808 ounces of silver, which is worth $3.00 at today's silver price per ounce. Unlike the Roosevelt dime series, there are some key dates in the series, which are outlined below from oldest to newest.

Key dates (worth more than $100 in lower circulated grades):

1932-D, 1932-S

Semi-Key dates (worth more than $15 in lower circulated grades):

1936-D, 1937-S, 1938-S, 1939-S, 1940-D

Standing Liberty Quarters

A much rarer design you might encounter when coin roll hunting quarters is the Standing Liberty quarter series. The design name refers to the beautiful image of Lady Liberty standing in a flowing dress on the obverse of the coin. The reverse features an eagle flying. An example is shown below which includes the three different variations of this design, as well as the mint mark location on each one.

"1917 D Standing Liberty Quarters Type 1." USA Coin Book. Accessed July 21, 2019. https://www.usacoinbook.com/coins/1994/quarters/standing-liberty/1917-D/..

Type I Standing Liberty quarter minted only in 1916 and 1917. There are no stars below the eagle. The mintmark is located to the left of Lady Liberty's right foot for all three types.

"1923 S Standing Liberty Quarters Type 2." USA Coin Book. Accessed July 21, 2019. https://www.usacoinbook.com/coins/2011/quarters/standing-liberty/1923-S/.

Type II Standing Liberty Quarter, minted from 1917 until 1924.

"1927 S Standing Liberty Quarters Type 2." USA Coin Book. Accessed July 21, 2019. https://www.usacoinbook.com/coins/2021/quarters/standing-liberty/1927-S/.

Type III Standing Liberty Quarter, minted from 1925 until 1930. The date is slightly recessed in an attempt to prevent it from being worn off during circulation.

The Standing Liberty quarter design was produced from 1916 until 1930. When you find a Standing Liberty quarter in circulation, you may encounter the same problem that you would with a circulated Buffalo nickel: The date will be worn off. The date is a raised part of the design on the standing liberty quarter, so it is not uncommon for circulated examples to be dateless. A dateless standing liberty quarter is worth only its silver content, which is .1808 ounces of silver, which makes it worth about $3.00 at today's silver price. A dated Standing Liberty quarter is worth a little more than its silver content: about $3.50. There are also some key dates in the Standing Liberty series, which are listed below from oldest to newest below.

Key dates (worth more than $125 in lower circulated grades):

1916*, 1921, 1923-S

Semi-Key dates (worth more than $40 in lower circulated grades):

1919-D, 1919-S, 1920-D, 1924-D, 1927-S

Barber Quarters

A design almost never encountered in circulation is the Barber quarter. Bearing an almost identical design as the Barber half dollar, this coin was named after its designer and mint director at the time of its production, Charles Barber. The Barber quarter design features Lady Liberty wearing a headdress on the front and an eagle with its wings spread on the back. An example is given below which includes mintmark location.

"1893 O Barber Quarters Early Silver Quarters." USA Coin Book. Accessed July 21, 2019. https://www.usacoinbook.com/coins/1922/quarters/barber/1893-O/.

Barber quarter design, produced from 1892 until 1916. The mintmark is located at the bottom of the reverse above the D in the words "QUARTER DOLLAR".

The Barber quarter design was produced from 1892 until 1916. Most Barber quarters that are found in circulation are very worn, making them worth only their silver value. A Barber quarter contains about .1808 ounces of silver, making it worth about $3.00 at today's silver value. In better condition, Barber quarters do command a slight premium, selling for between $3.50 and $4.00 each for common-date coins. Barber quarters have some key-dates, which are listed below from oldest to newest.

Key dates (worth more than $100 in lower circulated grades):

1896-S*, 1897-S, 1901-S**, 1913-S, 1914-S

Semi-Key dates (worth more than $25 in lower circulated grades):

1892-S, 1896-O, 1897-O, 1901-O, 1904-O, 1905, 1905-O, 1905-S, 1909-O, 1911-D

*A 1896-S Barber Quarter is worth upwards of $1000 in lower circulated grades. Because of this, I recommend that you get any 1896-S Barber Quarters that you find certified by a third-party

grading service. Please see **Chapter 8** for more information on third-party grading services.

A 1901-S Barber Quarter is worth upwards of $5000 in lower circulated grades. Because of this, I recommend that you get any 1901-S Barber Quarters that you find certified by a third-party grading service. Please see **Chapter 8 for more information on third-party grading services.

Profit and probability per box

Though many people do coin roll hunting because they enjoy it, there are few people who do solely to have something fun to do. Most people are looking to have fun and make a little money on the side. Due to this fact, I have broken down the average profit for a box of dimes. Please note that these are based off my years of results, so your results may be better or worse.

Washington Quarters: On average, I find 0 Washington quarters per box ($500) of quarters.

Standing Liberty Quarters: On average, I find 1 Standing Liberty Quarter every 25 boxes ($12500) of quarters.

Barber Quarters: I have never found a Barber Quarter in circulation, but the probability of finding one is about 1 every $100,000, or one every 400,000 quarters.

Profit Equation on Average

If you find 0 silver Washington quarter in a box of quarters, your profits will look like this:

0 Silver Washington Quarters x $3.00 net profit=

$0.00 net profit

This amounts to a $0.00 total net profit per box

As you can see by the above statistics, quarters are probably the worse denomination to coin roll hunt if you hope to make a profit. I don't really recommend quarters as a denomination to coin roll hunt for anyone.

Chapter 6: Half Dollars

Half Dollars are fairly complicated to coin roll hunt if you have little to no numismatic knowledge. Half Dollars, though fairly hard to acquire in roll or box form, are, by far, the most profitable denomination. Half dollars come in boxes of 1000, or $500. Half dollars come in $10 rolls, so there are 50 rolls per box. A box of half dollars weighs about 25 pounds, making it one of the heaviest boxes on this list.

Coins to Keep

When searching through half dollars, you want to keep every coin from before 1971. As with dimes and quarters, all half dollars from before 1965 are composed of 90% silver and should be kept. Unlike dimes and quarters, half dollars were produced with a 40% silver, 60% copper composition from 1965 until 1970.

Kennedy Half Dollars

The most common design example you will encounter is the Kennedy half dollar. Examples below illustrate a 90% silver Kennedy half dollar and a 40% silver Kennedy half dollar along with the mint mark location on both, which is illustrated with arrows.

"1982 D Kennedy Half Dollars Clad Composition." USA Coin Book. Accessed July 21, 2019. https://www.usacoinbook.com/coins/2926/half-dollars/kennedy/1982-D/.

Copper-nickel (75% copper, 25% nickel) Kennedy half dollar design, minted from 1971 until present day. The mintmark is located above the date and directly below Kennedy's bust.

"1968 D Kennedy Half Dollars 40% Silver Composition." USA Coin Book. Accessed July 21, 2019. https://www.usacoinbook.com/coins/2883/half-dollars/kennedy/1968-D/.

Silver (40% silver, 60% copper) Kennedy half dollar design, minted from 1965 until 1970. The mintmark is located above the date and directly below Kennedy's bust.

"1964 D Kennedy Half Dollars 90% Silver Composition." USA Coin Book. Accessed July 21, 2019. https://www.usacoinbook.com/coins/2879/half-dollars/kennedy/1964-D/.

Silver (90% silver, 10% copper) Kennedy half dollar design, minted only 1964. The mint mark is

located on the reverse to the left of the olive branch in the eagle's claw.

Kennedy half dollars began production in 1964, and are still being produced today. The Kennedy half dollar series does not contain any key dates, so Kennedy half dollars produced from 1964-1970 are only valuable due to their silver content. Kennedy half dollars from 1964, the only year the design was produced with a 90% silver, 10% copper composition, contain .36169 ounces of silver, making Kennedy halves from 1964 worth about $6.00 at today's silver price. Kennedy half dollars produced from 1965-1970 with a 40% silver, 60% silver composition contain .1479 ounces of silver, making them worth about $2.20 at today's silver price.

Franklin Half Dollars

The second most common half dollar series that you may come across is the Franklin half dollar series. These coins feature the Liberty Bell on the reverse and Benjamin Franklin on the obverse, hence the name. Below is an example which shows this design complete with the mintmark location.

"1952 D Franklin Half Dollars Liberty Bell." USA Coin Book. Accessed July 21, 2019.
https://www.usacoinbook.com/coins/2852/half-dollars/franklin/1952-D/.

Franklin half dollar design, minted from 1948 until 1963. The mintmark is located above the Liberty Bell on the reverse of the design.

Franklin half dollars were produced from 1948 until 1963. Like the Kennedy half dollar series, there are no key dates when it comes to Franklin half dollars. They are valuable because of their 90%

silver, 10% copper composition. A Franklin half dollar contains .36169 ounces of silver, making it worth about $6.00 at today's silver price.

Walking Liberty Half Dollars

The third half dollar design you may encounter when coin roll hunting half dollars is the Walking Liberty series. The Walking Liberty half dollar is widely considered one of the most beautiful coins in American history. It features a walking Lady Liberty on the obverse, which is where the coin gets its name. On the reverse, it features a sitting eagle. Below is an example of the Walking Liberty design which includes the two different mint mark locations that were used on this design.

"1917 S Walking Liberty Half Dollars Mint Mark on Obverse." USA Coin Book. Accessed July 21, 2019. https://www.usacoinbook.com/coins/2779/half-dollars/walking-liberty/1917-S/.

Walking Liberty half dollar design, minted in 1917 only. This design is unique to 1917 because

the mintmark is located on the obverse of the design, rather than the reverse. The mintmark is located below the words "IN GOD WE TRUST" on the obverse.

"1935 S Walking Liberty Half Dollars Mint Mark on Reverse." USA Coin Book. Accessed July 21, 2019. https://www.usacoinbook.com/coins/2806/half-dollars/walking-liberty/1935-S/.

Walking Liberty half dollar design, minted from 1916 until 1947. The mintmark is located on the lower part of the reverse to the bottom of the olive branch clutched in the eagle's claw.

Walking Liberty half dollars were produced between 1916 and 1947. Like the Franklin and Kennedy half dollar series's, a common date half dollar contains . 36169 ounces of silver and is worth about $3.00 at today's silver price. The Walking Liberty series does have some key dates, which are listed below from oldest to newest.

Key dates (worth more than $75 in lower circulated grades):

1916-S, Obverse Mintmark, 1921, 1921-D

Semi-Key dates (worth more than $30 in lower circulated grades):

1916, 1916-D, Obverse Mintmark, 1921-S, 1938-D

Barber Half Dollars

A much rarer design you may encounter while coin roll hunting half dollars is the Barber half dollar design. Named after Charles Barber, the head engraver of the mint at the time of this coins production, the reverse features an Eagle, while the obverse features a rather plain looking Miss Liberty. A design example, along with mint mark location, is shown below.

"1901 O Barber Half Dollars Early Silver Half Dollars." USA Coin Book. Accessed July 21, 2019. https://www.usacoinbook.com/coins/2730/half-dollars/barber/1901-O/.

Barber half dollar design, minted from 1892 until 1915. The mintmark is located directly below the eagle on the bottom of the reverse of the design.

The Barber Half dollar was produced from 1892 until 1915. Coins found in circulation are usually very worn, so they are valued only for their silver content. The silver content of a Barber half dollar is the same as the previous designs mentioned in this chapter: .36169 ounces of silver, which is valued at about $6.00 at today's silver price. Coins in higher circulated condition or in mint state are valued well above silver value. If you do encounter a coin in this level of preservation, I recommend you do further research as to its value using eBay or other online auction websites that give accurate market values. The Barber half dollar series does contain some key dates, which are listed below from oldest to newest.

Key dates (worth more than $100 in lower circulated grades):

1892-O, 1892-S, 1893-S, 1896-S, 1897-O, 1897-S, 1914, 1915

Semi-Key dates (worth more than $50 in lower circulated grades):

1896-O, 1904-S

Profit and probability per box

Though many people do coin roll hunting because they enjoy it, there are few people who do it solely for the purpose of having something fun to do. Most people are looking to have fun and make a little money on the side. Due to this fact, I have broken down the average profit for a box of half dollars. Please note that these are based off my years of results, so your results may be better or worse.

40% Kennedy Half Dollars: On average, I find 1-2 40% Kennedy half dollars per box ($500) of half dollars.

90% Kennedy Half Dollars: On average, I find 0-1 90% Kennedy half dollars per box ($500) of half dollars.

Franklin Half Dollars: On average, I find 1 Franklin half dollar every 2-3 boxes ($1000- $1500) of half dollars.

Walking Liberty Half Dollars: On average, I find 1 Walking Liberty half dollar every 7-8 boxes ($3500-$4000) of half dollars.

Barber Half Dollars: On average, I find 1 barber half dollar every 19-20 boxes ($9500- $10000) of half dollars.

Profit Equation on Average

If you find 2 40% silver Kennedy half dollars and 1 90% Kennedy half dollar in a box, your profits will look like this:

2 40% Kennedy half dollars x $1.50 net profit= $3.00 in net profit

1 90% Kennedy half dollar x $5.50 net profit= $5.50 in net profit

This amounts to a total $8.50 in net profit

Half dollars are obviously the most profitable denomination to coin roll hunt per box. I recommend that the first thing you ask when you go to a bank is if they have any half dollars. If you are looking to make a reasonable profit off coin roll hunting, I recommend that you coin roll hunt half dollars. Few banks have them constantly on hand, but if you can find a bank that can consistently order them for you, you are in business! I cover this ordering process to a further extent in Chapter 2.

Chapter 6: Dollar Coins

Dollar coins are much different than the rest of the coins on this list. If you come across silver dollar coins, you have hit the jackpot. By this you can understand that, while it is very rare to come across them, if you find silver dollar coins, you will make a lot of money. Dollar coins cannot be ordered in boxes, but banks occasionally have one or two of them or, if you are very lucky, an entire roll.

Coins to Keep

When coin roll hunting for dollar coins, you only want to buy what are called "big" dollars. The Sacagawea, Presidential, and Susan B. Anthony dollars, while attractive, are worth no more than their face value. There are two series of coins that you may encounter while coin roll hunting dollars that are valuable. Both series are just as hard to find as the other.

Peace Dollars

The first dollar coin you may encounter that has some value is called a Peace dollar. The name stems from its first year of production, which was a few years after World War I. The dollar was named the Peace dollar in hopes that a war like World War I would never occur again. A design example is given below, along with mint mark location.

"1935 S Peace Dollars Early Silver Dollars." USA Coin Book. Accessed July 21, 2019.
https://www.usacoinbook.com/coins/3328/dollars/peace/1935-S/.

Peace dollar design, minted from 1921 until 1928, and then again from 1934 to 1935. The mintmark is located on the left of the reverse above the eagle's tail feathers.

The Peace dollar was produced from 1921 until 1935 with a composition of 90% silver, 10%

copper. A common date Peace dollar is not worth much more than its silver content, which is about .77344 ounces. This is worth about $12 at today's silver value, but Peace dollars usually carry a bit of a collector's premium. They sell for about $18- $20 in circulated condition. The Peace dollar series does also contain some key dates, which are listed below from oldest to newest.

Key dates (worth more than $100 in lower circulated grades):

1921, 1928

Semi-Key dates (worth more than $50 in lower circulated grades):

1934-S

Morgan Dollars

The second dollar coin design you may encounter that is valuable is the Morgan dollar. This was named after George T. Morgan, the designer of the coin. Lady liberty's head is featured on the obverse, while an eagle with its wings spread appears on the reverse. Below is an example of the design complete with mintmark location.

"1889 CC Morgan Dollars Early Silver Dollars." USA Coin Book. Accessed July 21, 2019. https://www.usacoinbook.com/coins/3245/dollars/morgan/1889-CC/.

Morgan dollar design, minted from 1878 until 1904, and then again in 1921. The mintmark is located below the wreath and above the D in the words "ONE DOLLAR" on the reverse of the design.

The Morgan dollar design was produced

from 1878 until 1904 and then again for one year in 1921. Morgan dollars contain the same amount of silver as a Peace dollar: .77344 ounces, making them worth about $12 at today's silver value. As with Peace dollars, Morgan dollars carry a collector's premium, making them worth $20-$22 in average circulated condition. The Morgan dollar series is especially famous for its key dates, which are listed below from oldest to newest.

Key dates (worth more than $200 in lower circulated grades):

1879-CC, 1880-CC, 1881-CC, 1885-CC, 1889-CC*, 1892-CC, 1893, 1893-CC, 1893-O, 1893-S**, 1894***, 1895-O, 1895-S, 1903-O, 1903-S

Semi-Key dates (worth more than $100 in lower circulated grades):

1878-CC, 1882-CC, 1883-CC, 1884-CC, 1888-S, 1890-CC, 1891-CC, 1892-S, 1899, 1902-S

*A 1889-CC Morgan Dollar is worth upwards of $750 in lower circulated grades. Because of this, I recommend that you get any 1889-CC Morgan Dollars that you find certified by a third-party

grading service. Please see **Chapter 8** for more information on third-party grading services.

A 1893-S Morgan Dollar is worth upwards of $3000 in lower circulated grades. Because of this, I recommend that you get any 1893-S Morgan Dollars that you find certified by a third-party grading service. Please see **Chapter 8 for more information on third-party grading services.

***A 1894 Morgan Dollar is worth upwards of $750 in lower circulated grades. Because of this, I recommend that you get any 1894 Morgan Dollars that you find certified by a third-party grading service. Please see **Chapter 8** for more information on third-party grading services.

Profit, Probability, and Odds

As you can see, there is no profit and probability section for dollar coins. This is mainly due to the fact that, at this time, no bank-issued boxes exist for large dollars. As for the probability part of this section, consider yourself lucky if you have managed to come across even a single Morgan or Peace dollar at a bank. Many people who have been coin roll hunting for decades have never once encountered a Morgan or a Peace dollar in circulation.

Chapter 7: Returning your coins to the banks

When coin roll hunting, your biggest obstacle will not be acquiring coins to look through. Instead, the largest challenge you will face is returning your coins for cash. To simplify this process, I have outlined 3 different types of ways you can return your coins, as well as how you should structure the number and type of banks you have an account at.

Return type 1: Coin counter

This is definitely the easiest, most straight forward and least time consuming way to return coins you have already looked through. You simply dump the coins in to the machine, watch while the machine counts them, take your receipt, and then give it to a bank teller in exchange for cash. Be careful though. Many of these machines charge a fee if you are not a customer at the bank, and some of them charge a fee no matter what. The most important thing to avoid is the coin counting machines in grocery stores or pharmacies. These coin take huge chunks of your money no matter what. If you can, find a bank that has a coin counting machine that is free for customers to use. This will save you more time than you can imagine. It takes almost an hour to hand roll an entire box of coins, so the time a machine like this saves you will add up over a few years of coin roll hunting. In conclusion, the most important things with these type of machines is that it is free to use, that there is no fee, or else you are effectively losing the money that you made by coin roll hunting. If you can find a bank that has one of these, make it your dump bank, or the place you go to return the coins you have finished looking through.

Return type 2: Deposit bags

The only reason I mention this type of return is because one of the two banks I use has it. Deposit bags work like this: You put all the coins you want to return into the deposit bag, then you write the amount, in dollars, of the coins inside. It doesn't matter what denomination it is, meaning you can mix different denominations together inside of one bag. Though it may sound time consuming to count, say, $100 in pennies one by one into the bag, the whole idea is that you know how many coins you have gone through, how many coins you pulled out, and, therefore, how many coins now remain after you have taken out everything of value. This is the second best type of a return system, and this type always requires you to have an account at the bank you are returning the deposit bag to. Don't try to go to a bank that you don't have an account at and use their deposit bags; you will be turned away immediately.

Return type 3: Rolling coins by hand

This is by far the most time consuming, boring, and most difficult way of returning the coins you have already looked through. Do everything you can to try to find a bank where you can use one of the two above ways to return coins instead of rolling them by hand. If you do end up having to roll your coins by hand, do it for the moment, but always be in search of a bank where you can use one of the two above ways instead. When hand rolling coins, the most important thing is that you make sure each roll has the right amount of coins in it. To make sure of this, you should roll the coins you go through as your go through them. This means don't wait until the end when you are finished with a box or boxes of coins and have a big pile of coins to begin re-rolling the coins you looked through. When you go through a roll and don't find anything, re-roll it before moving on to the next roll of coins you are going to look through. This will save you the time of counting out whatever number of coins you need to have a roll of the denomination you are searching through, saving you hours. If you do take something out, make sure you replace it with another coin of the same denomination that has no value. I recommend using one roll of coins as a filler for other rolls you take things out of. When you get more coins, continue to use this "filler roll" until you have used it up, and then repeat the process. In conclusion, hand roll coins if you have to, but you are much better off if you are able to use either a coin counting machine or a deposit bag.

Chapter 8: Grading Your Coins

A coin's grade is one of the most important aspects when determining its value. The grade of a coin describes the wear and tear the coin has received since it was minted. Coins are graded on a scale of 1 to 70, with 1 being a disk of medal barely recognizable as the coin it once was, and 70 being a coins that is completely perfect up to 5x magnification.

Circulated vs. Mint State

Grading is also divided into two different categories: Circulated and Mint State. A coin that has circulated is a coin that does not have all of its details intact, no matter how small the wear might be. Circulated coins are graded on how much wear they have, and the scale for them spans from 1 to 58. Mint State coins are coins that do not have any wear on them that is visible under 5x magnification. Mint State coins are graded on a number of things, but the most important factor is the number of hits, or scratches, the coin has and, even more importantly, where the scratches are located. Mint state coins are graded on a scale of 60 to 70.

Defining each grade from 1 to 70

Poor-1: Almost no details are present. There are only enough details to make out what type of coin it is. The date and many large features are most likely not present.

Fair-2: Most defining features of the coin are present. All letters and legends will be completely worn away, but the reverse and obverse will still have their large features, though they will be very worn.

About Good-3: All defining features of the coin are present. The date is present, along with some of the lettering on the reverse and obverse.

Good-4: All of the features and all of the lettering on the coin are present, though still worn. The coin does not lack any major part of its detail.

Very Good-8: All features and lettering are present, and some smaller details start to appear in the very slightest.

Fine-12: Details on hair, wreaths and other intricate designs can be seen now, though still incomplete. All lettering is fully present, with little or no wear.

Very Fine-25: Lower parts of hair, as well as smaller details such as eyes and ears, are becoming clearer. While still worn, these details are starting to show through.

Extra Fine-45: Almost all details are present. There will be noticeable wear on the raised points of the coin, such as the hair and cheek.

Almost Uncirculated-50: There will only be wear on the very highest points of the coin. Virtually all details will be present, except for one or two tiny ones.

Almost Uncirculated-58: Only the tiniest amount of wear separates this coin from a mint state designation. The slightest rub on the highest details of the coin that is only visible under magnification keeps this coin from a mint state designation.

Mint State-60: The coin is marked by numerous scratches on grade sensitive areas, such as the cheek and hair. The strike may be weak and the eye appeal may be terrible, but there will be no wear on the coin, so all details are present.

Mint State-63: The coin has some scratches on grade sensitive areas, but much more of the luster on the coin is intact. The eye appeal of the coin is good, but not incredible.

Mint State-65: Most of the scratches on the coin are in the fields of the coin, or the least grade sensitive area of the coin. The eye appeal of the coin will be great, and almost all of the coin's original luster will still be intact.

Mint State-68: A few tiny hairlines can be seen underneath 5x magnification in the fields of the coin. All of the coin's original luster is present, and the coin looks incredible.

Mint State-70: The coin is perfect up to 5x magnification. The coin will show all of the intended detail and will have its luster fully intact. The eye appeal is spectacular as the coin is perfect!

What coins are worth grading?

It is not worth spending time separating

Fine-12 common date wheat cents from Very Fine-25 common date wheat cents, so I recommend that you only grade coins you are going to sell one by one. The coins that I recommend you sell one by one are listed in **Chapter 9** of this book. As you encounter more and more coins, you will learn more and more about grading, so persist in your grading efforts, even if you are frustrated when you begin attempting to grade coins, as it will get easier the more experienced you are.

Grading types of coins

It is obvious that the above definitions of grades are only overviews of each level and are not specific to types of coins. Many different types of coins are introduced in this book, and to go over each one in detail from Poor-1 to Mint State-70 would take far too long, so instead I am going to refer you to an app called Photograde which is an app created by PCGS (Professional Coin Grading Service). On the Photograde app, you can find specific examples of the different grades of every type of United States coin that has ever been minted.

Getting coins certified

If you have discovered a coin valuable and rare enough to warrant certification and grading by a third-party grading service, this section contains all the information you will need to know going through the process.

There are essentially two leading third-party grading services that dominate the coin-grading industry. There are other smaller, lesser-known third-party companies that provide certification and grading services, but these are numerous and rarely used. Therefore, it makes more sense to stick to the two leading grading services, PCGS (Professional Coin Grading Service) and NGC (Numismatic Guaranty Corporation). Each of these has separate systems and separate membership and grading fees. Outlined below is a general overview of the cost to join and submit coins to either grading service, as well as photographic examples of a coin certified by PCGS and a coin certified by NGC.

PCGS (photographic example shown below)

D, Tom, and Jsfmd. "US Coins." Coin Update. May 27, 2015. Accessed July 23, 2019.
https://news.coinupdate.com/pcgs-introduces-new-security-enhanced-holders-4852/.

Above is an example of a coin that has been certified by PCGS. Obviously, this is not a coin that would be found coin roll hunting, but you can still see what coins certified by PCGS look like.

Membership Options:

Silver ($69 annual membership fee): This is the basic membership, which includes no grading vouchers. This is the option you want to select if you are only submitting a few coins.

Gold ($149 annual membership fee): This is the

standard membership, which includes 4 grading vouchers. This is the membership to pick if you want to submit several coins throughout the course of a year.

Platinum ($249 annual membership fee): This is the premium level membership, which includes 8 grading vouchers along with other submission privileges. If you are going to be sending lots of coins in for certification every year, this is the membership you want.

Grading categories and fees:

Rarities: There is no coin too valuable to submit in the rarities grading category. The estimated turnaround is between 2 to 5 business days. The fees for submitting a coin in the rarities category are $300 as well as 1% of the fair market value of the coin plus return shipping and handling.

Walkthrough: The maximum value of a coin that you can submit through the walkthrough grading category is $100,000. The estimated turnaround is about 2 business days. The fee for submitting a coin in the walkthrough category is $150 plus return shipping and handling.

Express: The maximum value of a coin that you can submit through the express grading category is $20,000. The estimated turnaround is about 5 business days. The fee for submitting a coin in the express category is $65 plus return shipping and handling.

Regular: The maximum value of a coin that you can submit through the regular grading category is $3,000. The estimated turnaround is about 15 business days. The fee for submitting a coin the regular category is $35 plus return shipping and handling.

Economy: The maximum value of a coin that you can submit through the regular grading category is $300. The estimated turnaround is about 25 to 35 days. The fee for submitting a coin in the economy category is $22.

NGC (photographic example shown below)

"Certified Russian Coins Featured in UBS Auction 83." NGC. Accessed July 23, 2019. https://www.ngccoin.com/news/article/1294/Russian-coins/.

Above is an example of a coin that has been certified by NGC. Obviously, this is not a coin that would be found coin roll hunting, but you can still see what coins certified by NGC look like.

Membership Options:

Associate ($25 annual membership fee): This is the basic membership option. You receive no grading vouchers at this level. If you are looking to submit 1 or 2 coins at lower level submission categories, this is the membership option for you.

Premium ($149 annual membership fee): This the standard membership option. With this membership, you receive a $150 grading voucher with NGC. If you are looking to submit 1 or 2 coins in higher level submission categories, or you are looking to submit multiple coins at lower level submission categories, this is the membership option you should select.

Elite ($299 annual membership fee): This is the premium level membership option. With this membership, you receive $150 grading voucher with NGC with this option as well as other discounts related to submission. If you are looking to submit multiple coins at any level, this is the membership option for you.

Grading categories and fees:

Unlimited Value Walkthrough: There is no coin too valuable to submit in the unlimited value walkthrough grading category. The estimated turnaround is 24 business hours. The fees for submitting a coin in the unlimited value walkthrough category is $250 as well as 1% of the fair market value of the coin.

Walkthrough: The maximum value of a coin that you can submit through the walkthrough grading category is $100,000. The estimated turnaround is 24 business hours. The fee for submitting a coin in the walkthrough category is $150.

Express: The maximum value of a coin that you can submit through the express grading category is $10,000. The estimated turnaround is 2 business days. The fee for submitting a coin in the express category is $60.

Standard: The maximum value of a coin that you can submit through the standard grading category is $3,000. The estimated turnaround is 12 business days. The fee for submitting a coin in the standard category is $35.

Economy: The maximum value of a coin that you can submit through the standard grading category is $300. The estimated turnaround is 21 business days. The fee for submitting a coin in the standard category is $20.

Chapter 9: Storing your finds

Now that you have amassed quite a collection of coins pulled from circulation, you begin to realize that your current system of stacking them all over a desk or table is not going to work for much longer. Storing your coins to make sure they don't get damaged is one of the most important aspects of coin roll hunting. Below I have outlined, by denomination, how I recommend you store different types of coins.

Storage Materials

Throughout this chapter, I mention plastic flips. These are the staple storage item for storing coins. Most coin shops have some available for sale and they are available everywhere online. I recommend only purchasing these plastic flips unless they cost less than $0.10 each, which they should at most coin shops. A website I recommend online is www.amazon.com. Search "Plastic 2x2 coin flips", and the first option that comes up is the one you want to purchase. Try to buy them in the largest quantities possible, as the more you buy at once, the cheaper each one is. The most important thing when you are buying these plastic flips is that you make sure none of them contain PVC (Polyvinyl chloride), which will damage and destroy coins if they are left in a holder containing PVC for any extended period of time. By asking the dealer you are buying the 2x2 flips from or by looking through the item description if you are purchasing them online, you should be able to determine whether the plastic flips you are buying contain PVC or not.

Key-date coins

If you do find yourself with a key date coin, make sure to keep it in a 2x2 plastic flip that will assure it stays in the level of preservation it was in when you found it in circulation. Any damage to a key date coin will significantly lower its value.

Storage by denomination

Cents or "Pennies": If you have pulled many common date wheat cents out of circulation, don't bother to spend the extra money on specialized plastic rolls or 2x2 plastic flips. Regular rolls will work fine. Just make sure that you label each roll something that will stand out to you, so you don't accidentally return your finds to the bank! For older wheat cents, I recommend the same system, unless they are in exceptional condition. For wheat cents from 1909-1939 that are in high grades of circulation or in mint state, I recommend you use plastic flips like the ones shown below. These are available in large quantities for about 5 cents each and, for a coin in such a high grade, are well worth the purchase in the long run. Just make sure to buy in bulk! For Indian head cents and Flying Eagle cents, I recommend the same system no matter the condition. All Indian head and Flying Eagle cents are worth at least 20 times more than a plastic flip, so I recommend a using flips for these coins.

Nickels: The storage of silver nickels is the same as that of common-date or low-grade Wheat cents: Use paper rolls you can get for free from your bank! Silver nickels are worth nothing more than their silver content, so a few more marks or scratches will take nothing away from their value.

As for buffalo nickels, I recommend using paper rolls for both coin with no dates and coins with partial dates. For full date coins, it really depends on the condition of the coin. If you think the buffalo nickel you have found is worth well over $1, than it probably won't hurt to use a plastic flip, as long as you have bought these flips in bulk quantities! If you are lucky enough to discover either a Liberty head nickel or a Shield nickel, I recommend that you use a flip for both of these coins. Any coins of these designs will be worth far more than $1!

Dimes: Silver Roosevelt dimes should never be stored in anything other than a paper roll. These coins, even in uncirculated condition, are worth almost nothing more than their silver value. Even Liberty head dimes in incredible condition do not command much of a premium over their silver content's value. I recommend that you only use plastic coin flips for Liberty head and Barber dimes in truly exceptional condition or if you are storing a key date coin, as using holders otherwise is a big waste of money!

Quarters: Washington quarters are in the

same category as Roosevelt dimes: they should never be kept in anything except for the paper rolls that are free from your bank. The only exception to this rule is for the key dates in the Washington quarter series, which should be put in a plastic flip immediately. Standing Liberty quarters are a different story. If you do find a Standing Liberty quarter with a full date, it might be a good idea to put it in a plastic flip, as full date Standing Liberty quarters frequently command premiums far over their silver value. Barber quarters are worth no more than their silver value in worn condition, so, unless the Barber quarter you have found is in decent condition, it would be a waste of money to use a holder. Instead, you should use paper rolls for worn Barber quarters.

Half Dollars: Kennedy 40% and 90% half dollars should never be put in anything except for paper rolls. Anything else would simply be a waste of money. If you encounter Benjamin Franklin half dollars, you should follow the same rules for them as for Kennedy 40% and 90% half dollars: only use paper rolls. Walking Liberty half dollars can be a different story. If the Walking Liberty half dollar you have found is in condition better than Extra Fine, I recommend that you use a 2x2 plastic flip for it. Otherwise, use a paper roll. Barber half dollars are the same story as Barber dimes and quarters: if the Barber half dollar you have found is in decent circulated condition, above Very Fine, I recommend that you use a holder to store it. If the Barber half dollar you have found is in well circulated condition, don't bother to put it in a 2x2 plastic flip, as it is not worth anything more than its silver value.

Dollars: As Morgan and Peace dollars are the only dollar coins you would find in circulation with any real value, this is all this section is referring to. All silver dollars should be put into 2x2 plastic flips, as they almost always command a large premium, sometimes double or triple their silver value. For dollar coins in About good and Good condition, being put in holders is not as important as putting higher condition coins in holders. High grade dollar coins command large premiums, as said before, so it is imperative that they be put in holders that protect them from any further wear.

Chapter 10: Selling your coins

We have finally gotten to the last, and the most important step in making money coin roll hunting: selling your coins. Below I have outlined the four ways I recommend you sell your coins, as well as how to you should sell your coins, whether it be one by one or in bulk, to realize the most profit.

Why eBay?

I generally think that eBay is far and away the best platform for selling your coins. Millions of people view eBay every day, so you would have an enormous viewing audience as well as the widest range of collectors imaginable. When selling on eBay, it is easiest to put that you only accept PayPal payments. To set up and link a PayPal account to eBay, all you need is a debit card or a bank account. Also make sure that you review all of the fees that will be taken should your item sell, as PayPal takes a 2.9% fee + 30¢ and eBay takes a final value fee of 9% up to $50, the final value being how much your item sells for combined with shipping. To save money, also keep in mind that you only get 50 free listings per month before you have to start paying fees. For this reason, I recommend that you don't sell everything at once, as your profits will shrink if you do.

Finding "Sold" Listings

As with anything, prices in the coin market fluctuate year to year, month to month, and even sometimes week to week. Thus, it would not be wise to simply sell a coin at the same price that you sold one just like it for one year before. The easiest way to determine the current market value of a coin is on eBay. To do this, simply click the small icon that says "Advanced" next to the large blue search button on eBay's homepage. In the "Enter keywords or item number" type in the coin that you are looking for. I recommend that you include the denomination, date, condition, and any other important specifics that pertain to the coin you are trying to price. To see sold listings, click the box next to the words "Sold listings" in the category title "Search including". Once you do this, you can click the "Search" button. eBay only shows results from the last 90 days, so any prices you find should be accurate enough, though I recommend sticking to sales that have occurred during the last month. Make sure to look at multiple listings to get an average sale price, as looking at just one listing in order to determine what you should list your coin for can be misleading.

Bulk vs. One by one Cents or "Pennies"

When selling coins anywhere, but especially on eBay, you have the choice of either selling them one by one or as a bulk lot. In this section, I will outline which types of coins you should sell one by one and which types of coins you should sell in bulk. First off, let's start with wheat cents. There is no point in selling wheat pennies one by one, as no one will pay $3.50 shipping (The cost of shipping a bubble mailer) on a coin that is only worth 5-10¢. Wheat pennies should be sold in lots of 1000 and as unsorted, meaning all of your wheat cent finds, no matter how old they are, are combined into one

1000 count bag. I recommend charging $50.00 Buy It Now per lot of 1000. Also charge $7.25 for shipping, as 20 rolls of wheat pennies fits perfectly into a small flat rate box. The things you should keep out of this bag are older pennies in high circulated and mint state grades, as well as key dates. Key dates should be listed at slightly less that what other coins of the same date and condition are selling for. By slightly undercutting the prices of other eBay sellers, you are guaranteed to receive a much faster purchase and, thus, a much faster profit. This quick turnaround is worth the 5% to 10% you may lose by undercutting the prices of other sellers. Indian head cents, unless they are in good condition or are key dates, should be sold in 50 cent, or one roll lots, usually for about $45.00 Buy It Now along with $3.50 shipping. As for the key dates and high grade cents in this series, I recommend that you sell them in the same fashion as the early date and/or high condition wheat cents: At slightly less than the sale price of other coins in similar condition and with the same date. Flying Eagle cents should follow the above system.

Nickels

Silver, or "war" nickels should always be sold in roll form. These coins usually sell best when priced at somewhere between $34.00 and $36.00 a roll, plus $3.75 shipping. No date Buffalo nickels sell well when priced at about $7.00 per roll, plus $3.75 shipping per usual. Remember that, if someone wants to buy more than one, which often happens on eBay, it is best to ship them in a small flat rate box, as shipping in a bubble mailer, which is done by weight, is far too expensive. Full date Buffalo nickels should be sold in roll form, unless they are in very high grades or are key dates. Rolls of full date Buffalo nickels will consistently sell at about $22.00 to $25.00 plus $3.75 shipping. Liberty head nickels sell best in 5 coin lots with a Buy It Now price of $5.00 to $6.00, depending on the condition of the coins. High grade Liberty Head nickels and Shield Nickels should be listed as a Buy It Now listing at slightly less than the sale prices of other coins with the same date and in similar condition. High grade and key date Buffalo nickels should follow the above system.

Dimes

Roosevelt and Mercury dimes can be sold in mixed rolls for a Buy It Now price of $60 plus $3.75 shipping. I recommend that you separate any uncirculated Mercury dimes and then, once you have a roll, sell them for a Buy It Now of $70, with the extra $10 premium being added on for the condition of the coins. All key date Liberty Head dimes should be sold as a Buy It Now listing at slightly less than the sale prices of other coins with the same date and in similar condition. Barber dimes should be sold in roll form for about $140 a roll, unless they are in high grades in which case they should be sold for a Buy It Now for $5-$10. Key dates should be sold as a Buy It Now listings at slightly less than the sale prices of other coins with the same date and in similar condition.

Quarters

Washington quarters are in the same category as Roosevelt dimes: They should be sold in roll form. Washington quarters should be priced at a Buy It Now price of $120 along with the standard $3.75-$4.00 for shipping. Standing Liberty quarters are a very collectible series, so you can get quite a collector's premium over their silver value if they have full dates. Coins without dates usually fetch about $120-$125 per roll. Coins with full dates are easily sold for about $155-$160 Buy It Now plus $3.75 shipping. The $40 premium is the collector's value. Key date Standing Liberty quarters should be sold as a Buy It Now listing at slightly less than the sale prices of other coins with the same date and in similar condition. Barber quarters in lower grades command a slight premium of $20.00 to $25.00 per roll, with rolls of low grade Barber quarters selling for about $140 to $150. High grade and key date Barber quarters should be sold as a Buy It Now listing at slightly less than the sale prices of other coins with the same date and in similar condition.

Half Dollars

40% and 90% Kennedy half dollars command no premium over their silver value, so it makes the most sense to sell them in roll form. I recommend separating 40% and 90% halves to make it clearer for the buyer. A roll of 40% Kennedy half dollars sells for about $45.00 along with $4.00 for shipping. 90% Kennedy half dollars command about $120 per roll in addition to $4.00 shipping. Franklin half dollars fall into the same category as both 40% and 90% Kennedy half dollars: they should be sold in roll form. As they command nothing more than their silver value, a roll of Franklin half dollars sells for about $120-$125 along with the usual $4.00 shipping. Walking Liberty half dollars sometimes command a small premium well over their silver value. A roll of Walking Liberty half dollars usually sells for about $125 plus $4.00 shipping. Barber half dollars sell best in roll form only in deplorable condition for about $150 a roll along with the usual $4.00 shipping. With Barber half dollars graded higher than Fine-12, you will make the most money through selling them one by one on eBay. I recommend a Buy It Now price of between $10.00 to $12.00 as well as $3.50 shipping. As for key dates of both Walking Liberty and Barber half dollars, I recommend you list them for a slightly lower price than past sold listings in order to undercut other sellers and turn a quick profit.

Dollars

Both Morgan dollars and Peace dollars realize the most money if sold one by one. Peace dollars are worth about $22 along with $3.50 shipping from Good to Very Fine condition. Peace dollars in Extra Fine condition and above should be sold for about $28 along with the $3.50 shipping. Key dates should be sold as a Buy It Now listings at slightly less than the sale prices of other coins with the same date and in similar condition. Morgan dollars command slightly higher prices than Peace Dollars, selling for about $24 from Good to Fine condition and $28 from Very Fine to Almost Uncirculated condition. Uncirculated coins can go for well over $100, so I advise you to use past Buy It Now listings in order to determine how much you should list them for. If you have been lucky enough to encounter one of the very pricey Morgan dollars in circulation, I recommend that you sell it for a Buy It Now price, determining the price by looking through other eBay listings that have previously sold.

Photos and angles

The determining factor on eBay when selling items are the pictures you take. When taking photos, any smartphone will work, as you can access your camera roll when listing items on the eBay app. If you are selling one coin, take a photo as close to the front and back of the coin as you can while still getting the best resolution possible. If you are selling multiple coins, take pictures of the coins in the same way, zooming in as far as you can while still getting all the coins you are selling in one photo. The limit for photos on eBay is 12 per listing, 6 photos for the front of the coins and 6 photos for the back of the coins. If you are selling more than 6 coins at once, divide the number of coins you are selling by 6 and then group them by that number. If you are selling over 100 coins, which is how you should sell wheat cents, just take a large zoomed out photo of all the cents in a pile. It is not worth the effort to group them into lots and try to get a picture of each one individually. In conclusion, the most important factor when listing items on eBay is what photos you use on your listing, so, if you follow this section, you will have the best chance if having your items sell.

Shipping and packaging

Often the biggest challenge for anyone selling on eBay, especially if they are selling collectibles that are very desirable, is not actually selling the item, but shipping it. The first step is to buy envelopes to actually ship your items in. When shipping coins, I recommend a padded bubble mailer. These are available at almost every Post Office for $1.49, but you will get a much better bargain buying them from an office supply store. Most of them have 25 packs that cost about $15 each. This means that one bubble mailer, if bought at an office supply store, will cost you $0.60, almost two- thirds less than it would cost you at a Post Office. Amazon is an even better resource if you don't mind waiting a few days to receive the bubble mailers. A pack of 50 generally costs between $6 and $8 on Amazon.

The second step when shipping an item is to estimate the cost of shipping before the item sells.

On eBay, you will get an option to put in a flat rate for shipping, or let eBay calculate the shipping for you. You will also have an option for local pickup, but you should never use this option when selling collectibles, as it is unsafe, so I will not address that option in this book. The shipping calculator on eBay can be useful if you know exactly how much the item weighs and how big your package will be. You can figure out both of these specifications easily. First, find the width by using a ruler to measure the padded envelope. The weight of the coin you are shipping can be figured out through a little bit of internet searching. If you do not have access to the internet, almost all local libraries have computers available for use. Type in the name of your coin followed by the word weight and click on the first result. If the weight of the coin is given in grams, which it may be, you convert it roughly to ounces, which is the unit eBay uses, by dividing the weight, in grams, of the coin, or coins you are selling by 28. When selecting the type of mail service you want to use to ship the coin, select First Class mail. It is the cheapest mail service, but will still deliver packages within 3-4 days 95% of the time. Also make sure that you have selected a thick envelope when it asks for package type. Once all of this is filled out, you should get a price of somewhere between $3.50 and $4.00 shipping. If the cost of shipping is over $7.25, make sure to change the method of shipping to a small flat rate box, as a small flat rate box costs $7.25, no matter the weight.

Once your item has sold, you will encounter the third and final step: putting your package in the mail. If you prefer, you can write out the return address and the buyers address all by hand, and then walk to the Post Office to pay for shipping and to mail it. Some people prefer to do it that way. In my opinion, the easiest way to mail an item is to select the "Print Shipping Label" option that will appear next to your item after it has sold. Again, if you don't have access to printers, most libraries have one and will only charge 15 to 25 cents to print one page. Once you have printed out the label, slip your coin inside the padded mailer and seal it, and then tape the shipping label to the front of the package and put it inside a Post Office collection box, which can be found outside the post office as well as at other locations around your town.

Collecting your money

It is important to remember that you must have a PayPal account with a bank account linked to it in order to collect your money from eBay sales. On your eBay account, you can set your payment method to only PayPal, which is much less complicated than trying to collect credit card payments. If you do not know how to do this, search "Setting payment method on eBay" on the internet using the Google search engine and click on the first link, which should be the official eBay help website. Setting your preferred payment method will be explained in depth on this website. After you have received a payment for your item, the money will appear as pending in your account. If you click on the transaction, which will appear on your PayPal Summary page, it will tell you when the payment will be ready for collection. When you first start selling on eBay, payments will take 2-3 weeks to process, but once you have a few positive transactions, you will be able to collect payments the day they are sent. When selecting where you want to transfer your payments, select your bank account. It may take up to 2 days, but often the payment will be in your account the next day. Once it is in your bank account, it is up to you to do what you want to do with the money you have earned!

Coin Shops

I understand that not everyone has access to a computer or even a smartphone, so you may need to sell coins to a coin shop. Keep in mind that at a coin shop your profits will shrink. With lower price coins, especially coins like wheat pennies and buffalo nickels, your profits will be cut by a huge margin when compared to the profits you might make when selling on eBay. With silver coins, the margin will be much less when comparing eBay to a coin shop, so where silver coins are sold is not as important. Most people have a coin shop within their town and the can be found online or, if you have a phone book, in the yellow pages.

Coin Shows

Coin shows are one of the best places to sell coins in person without using the internet. There are thousands of coin shows across the United States every year, and the chances are high that there will be one in your area. At a coin show, multiple dealers set up tables and buy, sell, and trade coins. A coin show is much better than a coin shop, as you have sometimes hundreds of different people to sell to. Coin shows are sometimes the best place to realize good money for your coins as well as a great place to gain knowledge that will help you further in coin roll hunting and coin collecting, if you choose to enter the hobby.

Auctions

Coins that are sold at auctions run by professionals are usually rarities or in very high grades. I don't recommend selling your finds at an auction unless you do possess a true rarity, which is almost impossible to find in circulation. When you consign your coins to most auctions, you may have to wait months before the gavel will fall, so I recommend selling at one of the three above methods.

Chapter 11: 3 Ways to Save Money Coin Roll Hunting

Number 1: Keep your change. This may seem obvious to some of you, but there are many people who lose coins while hunting, especially when they use a coin counter. If you turn in a box of nickels that you removed 4 coins from and you get back $99.80, don't lose the 80 cents! Also, if you are hand rolling coins, make sure to keep track of the coins that you don't have enough of to make a roll! If you put it in your car or your pocket and forget about it, you are losing money! I recommend that you keep all of your extra change from coin roll hunting in a specific jar or cup in your house. If you are hand rolling coins, you can then exchange this nondescript change for the coins that you are pulling out of the roll. If you use a coin counter, at the end of the month or year, depending on how much you hunt, go to your bank and use the coin counter for all of your extra change. Remember, you want to save change by coin roll hunting, not lose it!

Number 2: Don't pay for empty wrappers. Almost all banks will give you empty wrappers for any denomination for free, so don't waste your money buying them online or at an office supply store! Not only will it take a while for the wrappers to get to your house, thus delaying your coin roll hunting, it will also steal your profits! If you need more wrappers, simply go to a bank and ask for them. Make sure to be specific about the denomination and the number of wrappers you need, as bank tellers tend to give you less rather than more.

Number 3: Keep track of your coins! When coin roll hunting, make sure you do it in a space where there is no way for any of the coins to go missing. If you go through coins in your car, make sure that you have a specific place for them. The more you scatter your coins, the better the chance that you won't collect all of the coins you have scattered. I recommend that you coin roll hunt in a place where you will have plenty of open space to keep your coins organized. This applies to the coins you remove from rolls as well! Many coin roll hunters have accidentally misplaced a great find in their return pile, only to realize their mistake after they had returned the coins! In conclusion, it is very important to keep yourself organized when coin roll hunting.

Chapter 12: Frequently Asked Questions

Should I keep proof coins?

For all of you that don't know, a proof coin is a coin struck by the mint specially for collectors. Proof coins are struck on polished planchets multiple times to deepen the strike detail and to give the coins a mirror finish. Occasionally, people who aren't coin collectors and don't know that these sets are collectible will spend the proof coins in the sets for face value. If you see a proof coin, you will immediately be able to tell the difference between it and a coin made for circulation. Though proof coins are certainly collectible, the only problem is that most proof coins you find in circulation may have some scratches or wear on them, making them much less valuable. As proof coins were struck to be perfect, it will be difficult to sell proof coins that have some imperfections. Though you may be able to profit in the slightest when you find proof coins in circulation, it is generally not worth the time and energy to try to sell them.

Should I buy a price guide?

When people find a coin while coin roll hunting, their first question is usually "What is it worth?". To answer this question, many people think they need to purchase price guide, either online or in a local bookstore. My recommendation is to not purchase a price guide. Price guides for coins cost about $16, and, when trying to maximize your profits from coin roll hunting, that is a very expensive purchase. Also, price guides mostly just give you a general idea as to whether or not your coin is legitimately rare, they don't really give market values. The best place to get an idea of what your coins might sell for is to go on eBay or other online auction sites and look for past sales of items like the one you are trying to evaluate. Not only is this much more inexpensive, as accessing online auction sites is usually completely free, but it is also much more accurate than looking up the value of a coin in a price guide.

How many banks should I open accounts at?

I recommend that you open accounts at two different banks. One of them should be the place you go to return to coins. This bank will be called your "dump bank". It is ideal if your dump bank has a coin counting machine that does not charge a fee for account holders. I explore this further in Chapter 5. The other bank you should have an account at is one that has lots of boxes of coins on hand for you to purchase. As mentioned in Chapter 2, it is ideal if this bank can order coins for you.

Should I open a safe deposit box?

If you have a collection of coins that you have pulled from circulation that is worth more than $2500, I recommend that you open the smallest safe deposit box possible. Many banks provide more than one size, and, the larger the box is, the more expensive it is. So, if you want to keep as much profit as possible, I recommend that you open a small safe deposit box at a local bank. In this box, you should only store higher grade copper coins and silver coins. Wheat cents, common date buffalo nickels and low grade, common date Indian head cents are not worth the cost of storage, so you can keep them at your home. Store silver coins and high grade or key date copper coins in your safe deposit box to protect them from theft. If you ever mention rare coins you have encountered in circulation, remark about them being in your safe deposit box, even if you have not yet opened one. The mere mention of it will discourage any potential thieves listening in on your conversations.

Works Cited

Websites used for pricing and general information

"PCGS Coin Price Guide: The Industry Standard for US Coin Values." PCGS. Accessed July 23, 2019. https://www.pcgs.com/prices.

"Electronics, Cars, Fashion, Collectibles, Coupons and More." EBay. Accessed July 23, 2019. https://www.ebay.com/.

"Certified Russian Coins Featured in UBS Auction 83." NGC. Accessed July 23, 2019. https://www.ngccoin.com/news/article/1294/Russian-coins/.

"PCGS Coin Price Guide: The Industry Standard for US Coin Values." PCGS. Accessed July 23, 2019. https://www.pcgs.com/prices.

"Type 2, No Rays - PCGS CoinFacts." PCGS. Accessed July 23, 2019. https://www.pcgs.com/coinfacts/category/nickels/shield-nickel/type-2-no-rays-1867-1883/673.

Bucki, James. "Learn All the Details about the Standing Liberty Quarter." The Spruce Crafts. April 25, 2019. Accessed July 23, 2019. https://www.thesprucecrafts.com/the-standing-liberty-quarter-specifications-4096404.

Plumer, Brad. "Cars in the U.S. Are More Fuel-efficient than Ever. Here's How It Happened." The Washington Post. December 13, 2013. Accessed July 23, 2019. https://www.washingtonpost.com/news/wonk

/wp/2013/12/13/cars-in-the-u-s-are-more-fuel-efficient-than-ever-heres-how-it-happened/?utm_term=.b320475e2b4a.

Johnson, David. "Gas Prices: See How Much More You Will Pay This Year." Time. June 12, 2018. Accessed July 23, 2019. https://time.com/5306658/gas-prices-calculator/.

Images (In order of appearance)

"Lincoln Wheat Cent." USA Coin Book. Accessed July 21, 2019. https://www.usacoinbook.com/coins/small-cents/lincoln-wheat-cent/.

"2017 P Lincoln Shield Cent Small Cents Copper Plated Zinc Penny." USA Coin Book.

Accessed July 21, 2019. https://www.usacoinbook.com/coins/6036/small-cents/lincoln-shield-cent/2017-P/.

"1943 D Jefferson Nickels Wartime Composition." USA Coin Book. Accessed July 21, 2019. https://www.usacoinbook.com/coins/998/nickels/jefferson/1943-D/.

"1901 S Barber Quarters Early Silver Quarters." USA Coin Book. Accessed July 21, 2019. https://www.usacoinbook.com/coins/1947/quarters/barber/1901-S/

"1907 O Barber Dimes Early Silver Dimes." USA Coin Book. Accessed July 21, 2019. https://www.usacoinbook.com/coins/1443/dimes/barber/1907-O/.

"1893 CC Morgan Dollars Early Silver Dollars." USA Coin Book. Accessed July 21, 2019. https://www.usacoinbook.com/coins/3262/dollars/morgan/1893-CC/.

"1935 S Lincoln Wheat Cent Small Cents Bronze Composite Penny." USA Coin Book. Accessed July 21, 2019. https://www.usacoinbook.com/coins/417/small-cents/lincoln-wheat-cent/1935-S/.

"1909 S Lincoln Wheat Cent Small Cents VDB Bronze Composite Penny." USA Coin Book. Accessed July 21, 2019. https://www.usacoinbook.com/coins/343/small-cents/lincoln-wheat-cent/1909-S/vdb/.

"1908 S Indian Head Cent Small Cents Bronze

Composite Penny." USA Coin Book. Accessed July 21, 2019. https://www.usacoinbook.com/coins/337/small-cents/indian-head-cent/1908-S/

"1864 P Indian Head Cent Small Cents With L Bronze Composite Penny." USA Coin Book. Accessed July 21, 2019. https://www.usacoinbook.com/coins/281/small-cents/indian-head-cent/1864-P/with-l/.

"1858 P Flying Eagle Cent Small Cents Large Letters Flying Eagle Penny." USA Coin Book. Accessed July 21, 2019. https://www.usacoinbook.com/coins/270/small-cents/flying-eagle-cent/1858-P/large-letters/.

"1939 S Jefferson Nickels Pre-War Composition." USA Coin Book. Accessed July 21, 2019. https://www.usacoinbook.com/coins/984/nickels/jefferson/1939-S/.

"1942 S Jefferson Nickels Wartime Composition." USA Coin Book. Accessed July 21, 2019. https://www.usacoinbook.com/coins/995/nickels/jefferson/1942-S/.

"1913 S Buffalo Nickels Indian Head Nickel - Mound Type." USA Coin Book. Accessed July 21, 2019. https://www.usacoinbook.com/coins/909/nickels/buffalo/1913-S/.

"1913 D Buffalo Nickels Indian Head Nickel - Line Type." USA Coin Book. Accessed July 21,

2019. https://www.usacoinbook.com/coins/911/nickels/buffalo/1913-D/.

"1883 P Liberty Nickels No Cents Liberty Head." USA Coin Book. Accessed July 21, 2019. https://www.usacoinbook.com/coins/873/nickels/liberty/1883-P/no-cents/.

"1912 D Liberty Nickels Liberty Head." USA Coin Book. Accessed July 21, 2019. https://www.usacoinbook.com/coins/904/nickels/liberty/1912-D/.

"1866 P Shield Nickels With Rays Early Five Cent Nickels." USA Coin Book. Accessed July 21, 2019. https://www.usacoinbook.com/coins/850/nic

kels/shield/1866-P/with-rays/.

"1870 P Shield Nickels Early Five Cent Nickels." USA Coin Book. Accessed July 21, 2019. https://www.usacoinbook.com/coins/856/nickels/shield/1870-P/.

"1972 D Roosevelt Dimes Clad Composition." USA Coin Book. Accessed July 21, 2019. https://www.usacoinbook.com/coins/1618/dimes/roosevelt/1972-D/.

"1946 D Roosevelt Dimes Silver Composition." USA Coin Book. Accessed July 21, 2019. https://www.usacoinbook.com/coins/1552/dimes/roosevelt/1946-D/.

"Mercury Dimes." USA Coin Book. Accessed July 21, 2019.

https://www.usacoinbook.com/coins/dimes/mercury/.

"Barber Dimes." USA Coin Book. Accessed July 21, 2019. https://www.usacoinbook.com/coins/dimes/barber/.

"1971 D Washington Quarters Clad Composition." USA Coin Book. Accessed July 21, 2019. https://www.usacoinbook.com/coins/2135/quarters/washington/1971-D/.

"Washington Quarters." USA Coin Book. Accessed July 21, 2019. https://www.usacoinbook.com/coins/quarters/washington/.

"1917 D Standing Liberty Quarters Type 1." USA

Coin Book. Accessed July 21, 2019. https://www.usacoinbook.com/coins/1994/quarters/standing-liberty/1917-D/.

"1923 S Standing Liberty Quarters Type 2." USA Coin Book. Accessed July 21, 2019. https://www.usacoinbook.com/coins/2011/quarters/standing-liberty/1923-S/.

"1927 S Standing Liberty Quarters Type 2." USA Coin Book. Accessed July 21, 2019. https://www.usacoinbook.com/coins/2021/quarters/standing-liberty/1927-S/.

"1893 O Barber Quarters Early Silver Quarters." USA Coin Book. Accessed July 21, 2019. https://www.usacoinbook.com/coins/1922/quarters/barber/1893-O/.

"1982 D Kennedy Half Dollars Clad Composition." USA Coin Book. Accessed July 21, 2019. https://www.usacoinbook.com/coins/2926/half-dollars/kennedy/1982-D/.

"1968 D Kennedy Half Dollars 40% Silver Composition." USA Coin Book. Accessed July 21, 2019. https://www.usacoinbook.com/coins/2883/half-dollars/kennedy/1968-D/.

"1964 D Kennedy Half Dollars 90% Silver Composition." USA Coin Book. Accessed July 21, 2019. https://www.usacoinbook.com/coins/2879/half-dollars/kennedy/1964-D/.

"1952 D Franklin Half Dollars Liberty Bell." USA

Coin Book. Accessed July 21, 2019. https://www.usacoinbook.com/coins/2852/half-dollars/franklin/1952-D/.

"1917 S Walking Liberty Half Dollars Mint Mark on Obverse." USA Coin Book. Accessed July 21, 2019. https://www.usacoinbook.com/coins/2779/half-dollars/walking-liberty/1917-S/.

"1935 S Walking Liberty Half Dollars Mint Mark on Reverse." USA Coin Book. Accessed July 21, 2019. https://www.usacoinbook.com/coins/2806/half-dollars/walking-liberty/1935-S/.

"1901 O Barber Half Dollars Early Silver Half Dollars." USA Coin Book. Accessed July

21, 2019. https://www.usacoinbook.com/coins/2730/half-dollars/barber/1901-O/.

"1935 S Peace Dollars Early Silver Dollars." USA Coin Book. Accessed July 21, 2019. https://www.usacoinbook.com/coins/3328/dollars/peace/1935-S/.

"1889 CC Morgan Dollars Early Silver Dollars." USA Coin Book. Accessed July 21, 2019. https://www.usacoinbook.com/coins/3245/dollars/morgan/1889-CC/.

D, Tom, and Jsfmd. "US Coins." Coin Update. May 27, 2015. Accessed July 23, 2019. https://news.coinupdate.com/pcgs-introduces-new-security-enhanced-holders-4852/.

"Certified Russian Coins Featured in UBS Auction 83." NGC. Accessed July 23, 2019. https://www.ngccoin.com/news/article/1294/Russian-coins/.

Made in the USA
Middletown, DE
28 July 2024